DO THE WORK!
REDUCED INEQUALITIES

COMMITTING TO THE UN'S SUSTAINABLE DEVELOPMENT GOALS

JULIE KNUTSON

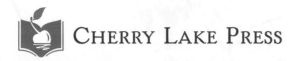

CHERRY LAKE PRESS

Published in the United States of America by Cherry Lake Publishing Group
Ann Arbor, Michigan
www.cherrylakepublishing.com

Reading Adviser: Beth Walker Gambro, MS, Ed., Reading Consultant, Yorkville, IL

Photo Credits: © Jaren Jai Wicklund/Shutterstock.com, cover, 1; © Riccardo Mayer/Shutterstock.com, 5; Infographic From The Sustainable Development Goals Report 2021, by United Nations Department of Economic and Social Affairs © 2021 United Nations. Reprinted with the permission of the United Nations, 7; © Raul Mellado Oritz/Shutterstock.com, 8; © Agarianna76/Shutterstock.com, 9; © casa.da.photo/Shutterstock.com, 10; © Jeff Whyte/Shutterstock.com, 13; © Syda Productions/Shutterstock.com, 14; © Ink Drop/Shutterstock.com, 17; © Arthur Bargan/Shutterstock.com, 18; © LightField Studios/Shutterstock.com, 21, 28; © SeventyFour/Shutterstock.com, 22; © Monkey Business Images/Shutterstock.com, 25; ©/Shutterstock.com, 26

Library of Congress Cataloging-in-Publication Data
Names: Knutson, Julie, author.
Title: Do the work! : reduced inequalities / by Julie Knutson.
Description: Ann Arbor, Michigan : Cherry Lake Publishing, [2022] | Series: Committing to the UN's sustainable development goals | Includes bibliographical references. | Audience: Grades 4-6
Identifiers: LCCN 2022005333 | ISBN 9781668909256 (hardcover) | ISBN 9781668910856 (paperback) | ISBN 9781668912447 (ebook) | ISBN 9781668914038 (pdf)
Subjects: LCSH: Equality—Juvenile literature. | Discrimination—Juvenile literature. | Income distribution—Juvenile literature. | Sustainable development—Juvenile literature.
Classification: LCC HM821 .K597 2022 | DDC 305—dc23/eng/20220210
LC record available at https://lccn.loc.gov/2022005333

Cherry Lake Publishing Group would like to acknowledge the work of the Partnership for 21st Century Learning, a Network of Battelle for Kids. Please visit http://www.battelleforkids.org/networks/p21 for more information.

Printed in the United States of America
Corporate Graphics

The content of this publication has not been approved by the United Nations and does not reflect the views of the United Nations or its officials or Member States. For more information on the Sustainable Development Goals, please visit https://www.un.org/sustainabledevelopment.

ABOUT THE AUTHOR

Julie Knutson is an author-educator who writes extensively about global citizenship and the Sustainable Development Goals. Her previous book, *Global Citizenship: Engage in the Politics of a Changing World* (Nomad Press, 2020), introduces key concepts about 21st-century interconnectedness to middle grade and high school readers. She hopes that this series will inspire young readers to take action and embrace their roles as changemakers in the world.

TABLE OF CONTENTS

CHAPTER 1

Meet the SDGs

Imagine a giant swimming pool. The pool represents a community. The water that fills it represents the total **income** earned by its residents. Now divide that pool into lanes, each holding people from different earnings groups. Would the lanes be divided equally?

This example from the Australian Council of Social Service shows that rather than lanes of equal width, the top 20 percent of earners would have lanes 5 times wider than people in the bottom 20 percent. In terms of how much people own, a person in the top 20 percent would have 70 times more space in our imaginary pool than someone in the lowest 20 percent.

According to a 2017 report by the British charity Oxfam, eight very rich men own as much wealth as the poorest half of the world's population.

Think about this from the perspective of a swimmer. In the highest income group, you have space to splash, float on a raft, and maybe even drive a remote-control boat. In the lowest income group, you might be pressed against a wall, bumping shoulders with neighbors. There wouldn't be room to jump in, practice your freestyle stroke, or dive for pool rings.

This **metaphor** shows what **inequality** is. It also illustrates its effects. At its simplest, inequality means that wealth and resources are unfairly **distributed** in a society. This unfair distribution results from histories of discrimination and exclusion that give some people privileges at the expense of others. These advantages might be rooted in things like ability, age, race, ethnicity, religion, or gender. Today, inequalities continue to affect people.

STOP AND THINK: *What forms of inequality do you see in your community? How are people and groups addressing it or not?*

REDUCE INEQUALITY WITHIN AND AMONG COUNTRIES

THE PANDEMIC
IS LIKELY TO REVERSE PROGRESS MADE IN REDUCING INCOME INEQUALITY SINCE THE FINANCIAL CRISIS

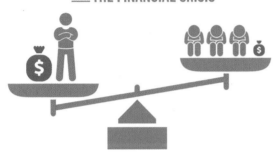

COVID-19
ESTIMATED TO INCREASE THE AVERAGE GINI FOR EMERGING MARKET AND DEVELOPING COUNTRIES BY 6%

THE GINI INDEX MEASURES INCOME INEQUALITY AND RANGES FROM 0 TO 100, WHERE 0 INDICATES THAT INCOME IS SHARED EQUALLY AMONG ALL PEOPLE, AND 100 INDICATES THAT ONE PERSON ACCOUNTS FOR ALL INCOME.

THE PROPORTION OF THE GLOBAL POPULATION WHO ARE REFUGEES HAS **MORE THAN DOUBLED SINCE 2010**

FOR EVERY 100,000 PERSONS, **311 ARE REFUGEES** (2020)

REMITTANCE COSTS
ARE AT AN ALL-TIME LOW AT **6.5%** (2020)

FURTHER PROGRESS IS NEEDED TO REACH THE 3% TARGET

IN 2020, 4,186 DEATHS AND DISAPPEARANCES WERE RECORDED ON MIGRATORY ROUTES WORLDWIDE

THE SUSTAINABLE DEVELOPMENT GOALS REPORT 2021: UNSTATS.UN.ORG/SDGS/REPORT/2021/

In 2020, the UN reported, "One in five persons reported being discriminated on at least one ground of discrimination prohibited by international **human rights** law."

According to the World Health Organization, an 18-year difference of life expectancy exists between high- and low-income countries. This difference has nothing to do with people's susceptibility to illness. Instead, non-medical, environmental factors are more likely to affect life expectancy.

What Are the SDGs?

The **United Nations**' (UN) 10th **Sustainable** Development Goal (SDG) "Reduced Inequalities" aims to make the lanes in our imaginary swimming pool more equal. How? By lessening income inequality, eliminating discrimination, and promoting the **inclusion** of all people. SDG 10 is one of 17 SDGs announced by the UN in 2015. The SDGs range from "No Poverty" (SDG 1) to "Climate Action" (SDG 13). Together, the SDGs address the most pressing and urgent issues facing our world today.

Some poor communities lack access to green spaces and hospitals.

Related Goals

Much overlap exists between the 17 goals. Often, action on one goal leads to progress on another. In this book, you'll learn about inequality and what's being done to fight it worldwide. You'll also discover how you can help address inequality at home, at school, and in your community. Let's get started!

The "Social Determinants" of Health

Experts in health care sometimes talk about the "social **determinants**" of health. These non-medical, environmental factors are beyond a person's individual choices. These factors impact health, well-being, and quality of life. They include access to healthy foods and safe housing. Social determinants are influenced by the places we live, learn, work, and play. An example might include a person who desperately needs to see a doctor but can't take time off work, find transportation to their appointment, or afford to pay their doctor.

To understand how factors beyond a person's control can influence their health, think about two communities located along a river. One is upstream, and the other is downstream. Big **structural** problems, like **institutional racism** and housing affordability, flow from the upstream community into the downstream community. These factors eventually impact health and become obstacles that are incredibly difficult to overcome.

CHAPTER 2

Why Do We Have Goals?

Setting goals allows us to transform an idea into a reality. When you name a goal, you express that it is something you want to achieve.

But it's not enough to simply say you want to do something. To actually *do* it, you need a plan. Some people use the acronym SMART (Specific, Measurable, Achievable, Relevant, and Timed) to guide the goal-setting process. For example, if you decide to learn to speak French, you'll plan to spend a certain number of minutes a day working on it. Maybe you'll aim to learn 20 new words a week. Your timeline to reach the goal of having a basic conversation in French might be 3 months. This is a SMART goal.

SDG 10 aims to end laws that discriminate against people based on factors like race, religion, gender, ability, or sexual orientation.

According to the UN, about 3.6 percent of the world's people are migrants, or people who live outside of the country of their birth. Many migrants send money to family in their home countries. They often have to pay a service fee for the transfer.

STOP AND THINK: *What goals do you have? How could the SMART method help you reach them?*

When a group or organization like the UN sets goals, people agree to take steps to work together to reach them. The SDGs are an example of this type of goal-setting.

To make the SDGs measurable, achievable, and relevant, each has specific targets and **indicators**. These targets are steps that need to be met in order to ensure progress on the larger goal. The indicators are a way of measuring success.

Here are the targets used to track progress on SDG 10:

- Reduce income inequalities.
- Promote universal social, economic, and political inclusion.
- Ensure equal opportunities and end discrimination.
- Adopt **fiscal** and social **policies** that promote equality.
- Improve regulation of global financial markets and institutions.
- Create enhanced representation for developing countries in financial institutions.
- Establish responsible and well-managed **migration** policies.
- Promote special and differential treatment for developing countries.
- Encourage development assistance and investment in the least developed countries.
- Reduce **transaction** costs for migrants who are sending payments to family in their home country.

CHAPTER 3

Do the Work! Contribute to the Goals at Home

How can you act to impact SDG 10 at home? Maybe it's reading a book that examines inequality and discussing it with a family member or friend. Or perhaps it is trying to understand the different forms that inequality takes. It might be making art that explains how inequality affects people and communities. There are so many actions you can take! Read on to learn more.

- **Read, Learn, and Share** — Whether investigating the roots of inequality, studying the **tactics** of the U.S. civil rights movement, or reading about Malala Yousafzai's work for educational equality, there's a lot to learn about why inequality

The UN reports that "despite some positive signs, inequality is growing for more than 70 percent of the global population."

exists and what you can do to change it. As you learn more about global inequality, consider the following questions:

— What different forms of discrimination do people face in today's world? How do these forms differ by country and region?

— Why do some people get to participate in politics, while others are excluded?

— Why is income inequality bad for all people, not just the poor?

— Why does racial inequality exist?

Ask a librarian for a list of books that tackle issues of inequality,
from personal stories to novels to nonfiction.

There are countless ways that you can become more informed about how inequality shapes our world and what can be done to end it.

- **Process** — Across the world and in all cultures, people use art to communicate their thoughts, ideas, and emotions. For example, the National Academy of Medicine in the United States hosts an "Art in Action" project, in which young people are encouraged to "Visualize Health **Equity**." Whether through painting, drawing, singing, or writing, find ways to express your views and educate others about inequality.

CHAPTER 4

Do the Work! Contribute to the Goals at School

There's a good chance that your school community includes diverse students from a range of cultural backgrounds and experiences. Talk to everyone! Break down barriers between groups. Discrimination and **bias** feed inequality. They often result from misunderstanding and lack of conversation. Open the doors to learning and understanding new people in the shared space of school.

- **Mix It Up at Lunch Day** — Visit the website of Learning for Justice to learn about how your school can host a "Mix It Up at Lunch Day." The aim of this popular program, which can be held any day of the year, is to encourage "students to identify, question, and cross social boundaries" by sitting

The first Mix It Up at Lunch Day was held in 2001.
In follow-up surveys of students who participated over the years,
97 percent said that their interactions were positive.

Are there places in your community that are not as accessible to someone in a wheelchair?

and talking with someone new at lunch. This can be a great first step toward building a more inclusive, safe, and welcoming environment in your learning community.

STOP AND THINK: *What benefit do you think that Mix It Up at Lunch could have at your school?*

- **Examine Spaces for Inclusivity** — As you walk around your school, think about the space from the perspective of students with disabilities. How **accessible** is the space for a student who uses a wheelchair? What can be done to address this? Make notes and share them with teachers and administrators.

- **Fundraise** — Whether a car wash or a walk-a-thon, you and your classmates can raise funds for organizations that fight inequality. Many charities work to reduce inequality, from assisting migrant families to helping people with disabilities find jobs.

- **Listen** — Across the country, activists work every day to reduce inequality. Talk with a teacher to see if you can invite an expert from your local community to visit your class. Topics that the guest speaker could address might include racial injustice, migrant rights, or fighting poverty. Find out more from this person about how young people can help address this challenge.

CHAPTER 5

Do the Work! Contribute to the Goals in Your Community

You can share many of the ideas for promoting equality at home and school with your community! Here are a few ideas for addressing inequality in your city or town.

- **Examine Spaces for Inclusivity** — Take a look at public spaces in your community. How easy is it for a wheelchair-bound or Deaf person to grocery shop or get on a city bus? What challenges might people with disabilities face in getting around in your community? Examine other spaces for diversity. Who is represented on your city council? Who is in charge of the police and fire department? Are these public institutions diverse and inclusive?

Accessible playgrounds are built with seven universal design principles in mind. These principles range from flexibility of use to the low physical effort to move a piece of equipment.

Playgrounds are a great place for children to meet and make new friends.

Making Play Accessible for All

Ava Villarreal was born with physical and mental disabilities. Doctors encouraged her mother to take her to parks and playgrounds for physical activity. They especially recommended swings to help Ava build balance and awareness of space. But Ava's mom couldn't find one that was accessible for her daughter. All of the swings required children to hold on, which Ava wasn't physically able to do. Her mother approached the leaders of their city of Palo Alto, California. Ava's mom told PBS that the leaders encouraged her to "design the kind of playground you think we would benefit from in our community."

And she did! For 7 years, she fundraised and worked with architects and designers to create the Magical Bridge Playground, which opened in 2015. Today, Magical Bridge draws 25,000 visitors each month. It is considered the most accessible playground in the United States.

- **Play and Meet New People** — You don't have to just "Mix It Up" in your school cafeteria! Take that same approach to the playground and park. Be welcoming, inclusive, and make some new friends whom you might not have otherwise met.

Write to elected officials. Your voice matters!

- **Advocate** — Let your elected officials know that you expect them to create and enforce laws that reduce inequality. From uncovering racial discrimination in policing to pushing for a fair wage for all, you can do a lot to pressure policy makers to create a more equal world for everyone.

[21ST CENTURY SKILLS LIBRARY]

Extend Your Learning

Background

The National Academy of Medicine's Young Leaders' "Art in Action" program, which is mentioned in Chapter 3, offers the opportunity to research and create art around issues of inequality. As the project organizers note, "These projects can use art to spark a dialogue about how our lives and health are shaped by everything around us, and to provide insight into how these factors support or hinder everyone's chances of living the healthiest life possible."

Take Action

The National Academy encourages young artists to consider the following as they create art in any form, from photography to painting:

1. What the world might look like when everyone has an equal chance to be healthy, safe, and happy.
2. How you would make sure you and your friends, family, and community all have the same chance to be healthy, safe, and happy.
3. How the social determinants of health shape your life and the lives of your family, friends, and community.

Further Research

BOOKS

Loh-Hagan, Virginia. *Racial Justice.* Ann Arbor, MI: Cherry Lake Publishing, 2021.

Smith, Elliott. *Income Inequality and the Fight Over Wealth Distribution.* Minneapolis, MN: Lerner Publishing, 2021.

Stanley, Joseph. *What's Income Inequality?* New York, NY: KidHaven, 2019.

WEBSITES

Goal 10: Reduce Inequality Within and Among Countries—
United Nations Sustainable Development
https://www.un.org/sustainabledevelopment/inequality
Check out the UN's Sustainable Development Goals website for more information on Goal 10.

The Global Goals of Sustainable Development
https://www.margreetdeheer.com/the-global-goals-of-sustainable-development
Check out these free comics about the United Nations Sustainable Development Goals.

Glossary

accessible (ik-SEH-suh-buhl) able to be accessed by all people

bias (BYE-uhs) prejudice against a group

determinants (dih-TUHR-muh-nuhnts) factors that affect the outcome of something

distributed (dih-STRIH-byoo-tuhd) shared or spread out

equity (eh-KWUH-tee) fairness in distributing opportunities and resources

fiscal (FIH-skuhl) relating to financial matters

human rights (HYOO-muhn RITES) rights that belong to all people on the planet, enshrined in the UN's universal declaration of human rights

inclusion (in-KLOO-zhuhn) the process of including and accommodating everyone

income (IN-kuhm) money received for work or through investments

indicators (in-duh-KAY-tuhrs) measurements of progress

inequality (ih-nuh-KWAH-luh-tee) situation in which some people have more rights or better opportunities than others

institutional racism (in-stuh-TOO-shuh-nuhl RAY-sih-zuhm) racism embedded in society's laws and operations

metaphor (MEH-tuh-for) a figure of speech that is symbolic and not literal

migration (my-GRAY-shuhn) the move from one place to another

policies (PAH-luh-sees) courses of action set by a government or organization

structural (STRUK-chuh-ruhl) at the base, root, core, or foundation

sustainable (suh-STAY-nuh-buhl) able to be maintained at a certain rate

tactics (TAK-tiks) methods or strategies

transaction (tran-ZAK-shuhn) the action of conducting business

United Nations (yuh-NYE-tuhd NAY-shuhns) the international organization that promotes peace and cooperation among nations

INDEX